YOU CHOOSE
BOOKS

STEALING
NAZI SECRETS IN
WORLD WAR II

AN INTERACTIVE ESPIONAGE ADVENTURE

by Elizabeth Raum

Consultant:
Dennis P. Mroczkowski
Colonel, U.S. Marine Corps Reserve (Retired)
Williamsburg, Virginia

D0450826

CAPSTONE PRESS
a capstone imprint

You Choose Books are published by Capstone Press,
1710 Roe Crest Drive, North Mankato, Minnesota 56003
www.capstonepub.com

Library of Congress Cataloging-in-Publication Data
Raum, Elizabeth.
  Stealing Nazi secrets in World War II : an interactive espionage adventure /
Elizabeth Raum.
     pages cm. — (You choose books. You choose: spies)
  Includes bibliographical references and index.
  Summary: "In You Choose format, follows the path of three World War II spies.
The reader's choices reveal the historical details from the perspective of a wireless
operator, a photo reconnaissance pilot, and a spy living in enemy territory"—Provided
by publisher.
     ISBN 978-1-4914-5861-7-1 (library binding)
     ISBN 978-1-4914-5934-8 (paperback)
     ISBN 978-1-4914-5946-1 (eBook PDF)
  1. World War, 1939-1945—Secret service—United States—Juvenile literature.
  2. Espionage—United States—History—20th century—Juvenile literature.
  3. Spies—United States—History—20th century—Juvenile literature. I. Title.

  D810.S7R38 2016
  940.54'86730943—dc23   2015019990

Editorial Credits
Mari Bolte, editor; Ted Williams, designer; Kelly Garvin, media researcher; Lori
Barbeau, production specialist

Photo Credits
Alamy: B Christopher, 54, Military Images, 102; Getty: Daily Herald Archives/
SSPL, 45, Fox Photos, 89, Haywood Magee/Picture Post, 96, Hulton Archive,
50, Hulton Archive/FPG, 100, Hulton Archive/Keystone, 36, 42, Keystone, 41,
Keystone- France/Gamma-Keystone, 66, Mondadori Portfolio, 12, Popperfoto, 74,
77; Glow Images/Heritage Images/Art Media, cover; Library of Congress: Prints
& Photographs Division, 8, Prints & Photographs Division/Henry Koerner, 6;
Newscom: akg-images, 1, 10, 15, 25, 83, Everett Collection, 30, National Archives/
KRT, 19, United Nations Information Office, 61; Shutterstock: Keith Tarrier, 70,
Peter Hermes Furian, 16, Richard Laschon, cover

Printed in Canada
032015   008825FRF15

TABLE OF CONTENTS

ABOUT YOUR ADVENTURE

YOU are living during World War II. The main battle is at the frontlines, but that's not where you belong. You're a spy.

In this book you'll explore how the choices people made meant the difference between life and death. The events you'll experience happened to real people.

Chapter One sets the scene. Then you choose which path to read. Follow the directions at the bottom of each page. The choices you make will change your outcome. After you finish one path, go back and read the others for new perspectives and more adventures.

YOU CHOOSE the path
you take through history.

More than 70 million people around the world fought in World War II (1939–1945).

THE
SECRET WAR

World War II began in September 1939 with the German invasion of Poland. The year before, Germany had used force to take control of Austria and large parts of Czechoslovakia. German power continues to grow.

Two days after the invasion of Poland, Great Britain declares war on Germany. Further attacks by Germany eventually lead to France, the United States, and the Soviet Union joining Great Britain's side. They call themselves the Allies. Those who side with Germany—mainly Italy and Japan—form the Axis nations.

TURN THE PAGE.

As time goes on, the war grows. Norway and Denmark are only two of the countries that fall under German control. Battles reach French soil. German planes begin bombing British cities. In September 1940 Italian troops move into Egypt and fighting begins in North Africa. By June 1941 Germany has invaded the Soviet Union. On December 7, 1941, Japanese planes bomb Pearl Harbor in Hawaii.

Around 350 aircraft were destroyed and 8 battleships, including the U.S.S. Shaw, were sunk or badly damaged during the attack on Pearl Harbor.

As though a world war isn't terrifying enough, the newspapers bring the fighting to your front door every morning. Battle wins and losses are described in detail. Locations of dropped bombs or overrun towns and villages are revealed. The number of soldiers killed and wounded grows every day. You can't sit by and do nothing. But the frontlines aren't for you.

There's another war, a secret war, which no one reads about. But the signs are everywhere. Newspapers and signs warn civilians to keep their mouths shut. From the beginning, both Allied and Axis leaders have gathered reports on the enemy's strength and positions. To do that, they use spies.

TURN THE PAGE.

Thousands of women enlisted as radio operators.

Some spies actually sneak into offices and military headquarters and steal official reports and war plans. But most spies are pilots, photo interpreters, code breakers, and agents working undercover. They live and work in occupied cities and observe the enemy close up. They take pictures of secret locations or interpret the photos. They intercept and decipher coded messages from the enemy.

These spies work in secret, rarely revealing exactly what they do or how they do it. It is dangerous work. A mistake can cost you your life. It's no job for thrill or fame seekers. And chances are that no one will read about your heroic deeds. But your work will help the Allies win this war. What kind of spy are you?

TO STEAL SECRETS FROM JAPANESE LIVING IN THE PHILIPPINES, **TURN TO PAGE 13.**

TO RELAY SECRETS FROM INSIDE OCCUPIED PARIS AS A WIRELESS OPERATOR, **TURN TO PAGE 43.**

TO FLY A SPY PLANE AS A MILITARY PHOTOGRAPHER, **TURN TO PAGE 71.**

Military outposts in Hawaii made the United States'
presence in the Pacific possible.

CHAPTER 2

UNDERCOVER

The palm trees, sandy beaches, and coral reefs of Hawaii are your home. Your parents are Japanese immigrants, but you are an American. To other Japanese you are *Nisei*, the first generation born away from the Japanese homeland. You are fluent in both Japanese and English and are comfortable in both cultures.

As a student at Honolulu's McKinley High School, you are required to join the ROTC, a military training program. Training both the mind and body are important. Your principal stresses the importance of involvement. You are charged with guarding important military areas on the island of Oahu.

13

TURN THE PAGE.

You graduate as a cadet officer, but don't think anything more of military service. After graduation you begin work for a company that manages sugar cane plantations. It's not very interesting work, but you try to convince yourself that it's important to someone.

One day, though, you get a call from one of your ROTC officers. "Would you consider joining a special branch of the U.S. Army?" he asks. "Your knowledge of Japanese language and culture will be an asset. The army wants to keep an eye on overseas activity." As a bonus, he tells you that the assignment involves travel to interesting places.

You jump at the chance. Arthur Komori, another *Nisei*, signs up with you. You attend the Counter Intelligence School in Carlisle, Pennsylvania. It's part of the United States Army War College.

You study languages and codes. The Japanese merchant fleet uses a code called JN25. The Japanese Navy uses a new code known as Purple. Code-breakers in Washington, D.C. struggled to decipher the code.

The college has built a model of the Purple machine. It consists of two typewriters, a rotor, and a 25-character alphabet. The rotor scrambles the letters every day. Only someone with the secret key can decipher the messages.

The German's code machine was known as Enigma.

TURN THE PAGE.

You and Komori are the very first Japanese-Americans to work for the Counter Intelligence Corps (CIC). On April 7, 1941, you board a transport ship headed toward Manila, the capital city in the Philippines. The Philippine islands are an American territory.

Your mission is to integrate with the Japanese citizens in Manila. You travel undercover as civilian deck hands. None of the other passengers or crew, who are also mostly civilians, know that you work for the U.S. Army.

On April 21 you are summoned to the captain's office. Two men in civilian clothes are there. They introduce themselves as Major Nelson Raymond, your CIC chief, and Agent Grenfall Drisko, who will be your contact.

Raymond gives you a cover story to use once you land. People must believe you are loyal to Japan, even though you were born in the United States. Only Major Raymond and Agent Drisko will know that you are CIC agents.

When you reach Manila, the major gives you a brief tour. He hands you keys to a mailbox at the Central Post Office in Manila. "It's registered under a Filipino name, Sixto Borja. Check twice daily for instructions and to drop off your intelligence reports." You and Komori are instructed to register at different hotels.

TO REGISTER AT THE TOYO HOTEL, **TURN TO PAGE 18.**

TO REGISTER AT THE NISHIKAWA HOTEL, **TURN TO PAGE 22.**

You register at the Toyo Hotel and find a job as an English teacher at the Japanese Cultural Hall in Manila. "I'm dodging the U.S. draft," you brag. This impresses your Japanese clients. Leading Japanese residents come to the Cultural Hall to visit with likeminded people. In time they come to see you as one of them.

You use your social time at the Hall to befriend the chief of the Japanese News Agency, the chief of the Japanese Tourist Bureau, the Japanese Consul General (who represents the government of Japan in the Philippines), and

others. You draw them into conversations that hint at Japanese military plans. One newspaper reporter reveals the likely route of Japanese forces when they land in British-controlled Singapore. You write reports and deliver them to the post office box.

On December 7, 1941, Japanese planes bomb the American naval base in Pearl Harbor. Your new "friends" rejoice. You play along, but worry in secret about your friends and family. There's no way to contact anyone back home without looking suspicious. You are restless at night, afraid of what you might say in your sleep. If anyone discovers that you are an undercover agent, things could get dangerous.

More than 2,400 Americans lost their lives during the attack on Pearl Harbor.

TURN THE PAGE.

You're listening to news reports at the Japanese New Agency. Someone has just said a toast to the Japanese emperor and you're all raising your glasses when the door flies open. Filipino police, with bayonets drawn, force everyone into a waiting bus. You and the rest of the Japanese Cultural Hall members are taken to Bilibid Prison and locked up. It's where civilian prisoners-of-war are kept. The buildings are not well insulated and have a dampness that doesn't go away. You itch constantly from lice, bedbugs, and mosquito bites.

It's an anxious time. Your original cover story sounds weak when you think about it. You test out different cover stories in your head. What if the members of the Japanese Cultural Hall find out that you are a secret agent? Will Major Raymond rescue you?

It's Agent Drisko who saves the day. "It's starting," he says grimly. The next day President Roosevelt announces the United States is at war with Japan. It's time for you to leave.

You join the CIC staff on a boat to Bataan, a mountainous peninsula on the southern part of the island. From there you go to Corregidor, a fortified island off the tip of the peninsula. Massive gun installations protect the coast, and tunnels below the surface are home to a hospital, supply depot, and offices. General Douglas MacArthur, the famous American commander, has his headquarters there.

21

"We need someone familiar with the Purple machine," the chief of staff says. "But General MacArthur also needs a translator."

TO WORK ON THE PURPLE MACHINE, TURN TO PAGE 26.

TO TRANSLATE FOR MACARTHUR, TURN TO PAGE 27.

You take a room at the Nishikawa Hotel and begin life in the Philippines as a sales rep for Sears and Roebuck Company. It's an effective cover. You have memorized their sales brochures and have several sales pitches prepared.

You start spending time at the Japanese Club, where prominent Japanese businessmen socialize. You record any information of value and drop it in the post office box. You also work part-time in the hotel as a clerk. This job lets you inspect the passports and documents of Japanese visitors.

There is much cheering at the Japanese Club after the Pearl Harbor bombings. Around 200 aircraft are destroyed and 21 Navy ships, including a number of massive battleships, are sunk. You struggle to hide your true feelings as the men around you celebrate. You resolve to fight back any way you can.

Now that the United States is at war with Japan, all Japanese citizens must report their assets to authorities. Many seek your help filling out the forms. You ask additional questions about their military background and pass the information on to Major Raymond.

Tensions are rising. One day all Japanese are ordered to report to the police station. You are taken to the Japanese Club, which has become a detention center. Because you are American, you are allowed to come and go as you please.

Someone must go to Manila for supplies. It's a dangerous mission. Local Filipino gangs attack anyone who looks Japanese. They don't check passports or ask questions first.

23

TO GO FOR FOOD, TURN TO PAGE 24.

TO STAY AT THE CLUB, TURN TO PAGE 28.

You leave the detention center and rush to your hotel to gather some clothing and food. You're about to leave your room when three Filipino Secret Service agents arrest you on suspicion of being a Japanese spy. You? A Japanese spy? You almost laugh. But the truth isn't any less incriminating.

The police arrest you and send you to Bilibid Prison. You feel chills as you pass through the tall white gate of the prison.

Agent Drisko is able to free you a few days later. The battle has come to Manila—Japanese bombs are falling on the city. Drisko accompanies you to Corregidor, where the rest of the CIC staff is waiting. General Douglas MacArthur has moved his headquarters into underground tunnels on the rocky, heavily fortified island.

"MacArthur needs a translator," the chief says. "I also need a translator to return to Bataan. The fighting is intense, and someone has to translate any enemy documents we find and interview any prisoners that we take."

General Douglas MacArthur retired from the U.S. Army in 1937. He returned to active duty after the attack on Pearl Harbor.

TO JOIN MACARTHUR'S STAFF, TURN TO PAGE 27.

TO RETURN TO BATAAN, TURN TO PAGE 35.

You've always been good at solving puzzles, and the model Purple machine back in Washington seemed like a challenge. But before you can start, you receive word that the Japanese have changed all their codes. "The machine is useless now," the chief says, frustrated.

The danger on Corregidor increases. Japanese forces are getting closer. Allied troops are fighting in Borneo, New Guinea, and Singapore. The fortified caves seem less safe every day. Finally you receive orders: "Destroy the Purple machine and evacuate." The first evacuation ship is going to Java, an island north of Australia. If you wait, you can go directly to Australia. Leaving sooner means safety on land—but the trip at sea might be risky too.

26

TO GO TO JAVA, TURN TO PAGE 31.

TO WAIT, TURN TO PAGE 32.

As America's most famous general, MacArthur is one of your heroes. He has spent his entire life in the army, and is very familiar with the Philippines. He's got a big ego, but there's no denying his talent. In July 1941 President Roosevelt named MacArthur commander of all U.S. Army Forces in the Far East.

But there's only so much the famous commander can do. Japanese attacks are increasing. General MacArthur is forced to evacuate to Australia.

TURN TO PAGE 37.

The streets are dangerous. It's safest to travel after dark. Two others volunteer to get food. At nightfall you go to the hotel and begin collecting your things. As you're finishing up, there's a knock at the door. Who could it be at this hour?

It's Sammy Jones, a businessman you met at the Japanese Club. His mother is Japanese; his father is Canadian. "Look, don't be alarmed, I'm not going to say anything to anyone else, but I don't think you're as Japanese as you'd like everyone to believe," he says.

His name and his Canadian passport guarantee his safety as long as the Japanese don't invade the Philippines. He invites you to stay at his apartment. You tell him you'll think about it. It's a generous offer. You could be safe and relatively comfortable.

The longer you think, though, the more his words start to eat at you. You begin to worry that other people might suspect you. The city starts to feel like a prison cell. You jump whenever you hear a noise. You strain to listen whenever you hear voices. Are they talking about you?

The next night you slip out to check the post office box for instructions. There's a note: "Report to the east docks at 2:00 a.m." What a relief! Your belongings are still packed. It's easy to lay low until nightfall. At the dock Drisko directs you to a boat leaving for the Bataan Peninsula. The entire CIC staff has moved to the mountainous jungle region.

"We need translators here and on Corregidor," the chief says.

29

TURN THE PAGE.

Corregidor is a fortified island two miles from Bataan where General MacArthur has established headquarters. On Corregidor you'll translate documents for MacArthur. On Bataan you'll interrogate prisoners, collect enemy documents, and go on scouting missions.

30

U.S. Army headquarters in a fortified tunnel in Corregidor

TO GO TO CORREGIDOR,
TURN TO PAGE 33.

TO STAY ON BATAAN,
TURN TO PAGE 35.

You reach Java in mid-February. On February 25, 1942, pilots spot two Japanese convoys on their way to the island. Allied bombers fail to stop them, and there's no time to evacuate. The battle begins two days later. The Japanese sink two Dutch cruisers, four destroyers, the American cruiser USS *Houston*, and the Australian ship *Perth*. They take about 2,700 Allied prisoners. You're one of them.

TURN TO PAGE 41.

On March 18 you board the USS *Perch*, a submarine bound for Australia. The sub is hot and crowded. You stay below the surface until after dark, trying to avoid enemy ships. But one evening the sub surfaces between three enemy destroyers. The *Perch* dives deep. The destroyers fire depth charges all night. Explosions rattle the sub. You prepare to die—your imagination runs wild with the ways you could perish at sea—but the submarine manages to escape.

At last you reach the Australian city of Melbourne. Your new task is to decipher JN25 messages from the Japanese merchant fleet. The code consists of 33,000 5-digit code groups. It is hard work, but it pays off. You help disrupt Japanese shipping, and that helps end the war.

THE
-END-

To follow another path, turn to page 11.
To read the conclusion, turn to page 101.

In Corregidor you're assigned to Detachment 6, Second Signal Service Company. You'll decipher Japanese messages. It's not hard work, but it does require 16- to 20-hour days in underground tunnels. You monitor Japanese air force communications. They're not even using coded language. It's straight translation, and you're able to warn Allied troops when and where to expect attacks. Japanese planes bomb the rocky island, trying to destroy the tunnels. Your desk shakes. It's hard to concentrate.

Japanese attacks increase. General MacArthur moves his headquarters to Australia. Before he leaves, he urges you to leave on the next transport. The Japanese will not be kind to *Nisei*, especially if they discover that you are an undercover agent. You'll be safe in Australia, and you can continue your work there.

TURN THE PAGE.

A civilian named Clarence Yamagata has been helping you with the translations. He's become a friend. Clarence's wife and small children still live in Japan. If he's captured the Japanese will threaten his family. They could be in great danger. Unfortunately, there's not enough room on the plane for both of you.

34

TO GO TO AUSTRALIA, TURN TO PAGE 37.

TO LET CLARENCE GO, TURN TO PAGE 38.

American troops are fighting a life or death battle on Bataan. You can help. You build a makeshift bamboo and grass shed to serve as headquarters. You go through enemy documents as quickly as possible. One warns of an upcoming attack, and your translation helps to squash it. Sometimes you travel to the front lines to collect papers off dead enemy soldiers. It's grisly but necessary. Japanese soldiers keep detailed diaries that include information about their tactics, weapons, and movements. You try not to look at their faces as you pick their pockets.

Supplies are running low and enemy attacks are increasing. On April 9 Bataan falls to the enemy. You are among the 76,000 Filipino and American troops taken prisoner. You're expected to march 65 miles to the prisoner camps.

35

TURN THE PAGE.

Around 76,000 prisoners were forced to take part in the Bataan Death March.

It's a long march without food or water, and it's hot. It's at least a five-day walk. Anyone who falls behind is beaten. Those too weak to walk are stabbed with bayonets. As a *Nisei* you are singled out for the roughest treatment. Like thousands of others, you die on what becomes known as the Bataan Death March.

THE
−END−

To follow another path, turn to page 11.
To read the conclusion, turn to page 101.

MacArthur strongly suggests you go. You board a patched-up training plane. "We think it will fly," the pilot says. You can't tell if he's joking.

The plane flies through the Japanese blockade without a scratch. Then a B-25 bomber takes you to another island, Mindanao. The pilot flies just above the waves. It's scary to be so close to crashing. "Enemy planes can't see us when we fly a few feet above our shadow," the pilot explains when he sees your face. "It's like we're invisible!"

You'd rather be invincible. You grip the seat and stare at the horizon until you've safely landed. On the runway you take a deep breath. You've made it. Now you can continue your code work from the safety of Australian soil.

THE
-END-

To follow another path, turn to page 11.
To read the conclusion, turn to page 101.

You give Clarence your place. After he leaves, you help destroy files and records before receiving new orders: "If possible, go undercover in the Japanese army. Funnel any documents to guerrilla forces fighting in the hills."

On May 6, 1942, Japanese forces reach the island. The military police, the *Kempeitai*, begin interrogations right away. "What were you doing with the Americans?" they ask.

"They took me from a detention center and used me as an interpreter."

38 Even under torture you never change your story. The *Kempeitai* speak to you in harsh tones. But on the third day you get a friendly officer. He makes small talk and gives you a piece of chocolate. Then he casually asks you how much the army paid you as an interpreter.

TO ANSWER RIGHT AWAY, GO TO PAGE 39.

TO THINK OF A LIE, TURN TO PAGE 40.

The Japanese officer's kindness catches you off guard, and you answer before thinking. As soon as the words are spoken, you know you've made a mistake. The U.S. Army would not pay someone they took from detention. Now the officer knows that your cover story is false. He reports you to the chief interrogator who beats you and burns you with cigarettes. Still, you refuse to admit you are an American.

TURN TO PAGE 41.

"Pay?" you say. "They gave me food and a bed. That's all." Saying you were paid would have told the officer that you were employed by the U.S. military. You've passed this test.

Finally they give up questioning and make you an officer's servant. You eventually gain access to the entire headquarters. As you clean, you memorize papers and maps. Then one night you slip out of the Japanese camp.

You join a band of Filipino freedom fighters who help you pass information to the U.S. Army.

Several months later an American guerrilla team rescues you. You spend the rest of the war in Australia interrogating Japanese prisoners and translating for Allied generals.

THE
-END-

To follow another path, turn to page 11.
To read the conclusion, turn to page 101.

*Japanese soldiers marching defenders
in Corregidor to prison camps*

The conditions in the prisoner of war camp
are brutal. As a *Nisei*, you are seen as a traitor.
Every day you are in extreme danger of death.
Japanese guards find the smallest reasons to
beat you or withhold food, water, or medical
care. You want to return to Hawaii. But it is
not to be. You die in the camp, two years before
the war ends.

**THE
-END-**

To follow another path, turn to page 11.
To read the conclusion, turn to page 101.

Germany occupied Paris on June 14, 1940. More than 2 million Parisians had already fled the city.

CHAPTER 3

THE WIRELESS OPERATOR

Father listens to the radio and reads the newspaper daily to stay updated on the war. On September 3, 1939, England and France declare war on Germany. "We must return to England," he announces one morning over breakfast. "I fear that we won't be safe in France."

It takes a few months for Father to arrange his business affairs. In March 1940 you cross the English Channel for London. Father's predictions are right. In mid-June German troops enter Paris.

You want to stop the Germans and free France, so you join the Women's Auxiliary Air Force (WAAF) and train as a wireless operator.

TURN THE PAGE.

The wireless is a radio that uses Morse code. You memorize the system of dots and dashes and learn how to tap them out quickly. Your radio can send and receive messages from 500 miles away.

Your skills as a wireless operator combined with your French language skills attract the attention of Britain's Special Operations Executive (SOE). "We need you," the SOE chief says. "The work is vitally important, but it is dangerous. We estimate that wireless operators have about a 50/50 chance to survive." That doesn't scare you. The men on the front lines are at risk too. In February 1943 you report for special ops training.

You study Nazi uniforms and ranks so that you can identify the enemy. You try to learn the art of killing. "This is war, not sport," the instructor says after one botched attempt to "kill" a fellow trainee.

The SOE sends agents into France by parachute drop. You hate the parachute training. On your first jump, you drift backward and are caught in a tree. You dangle 30 feet above the ground trying to untangle yourself. Eventually, you master parachuting enough to pass.

The Women's Auxiliary Air Force was formed in June 1939.

TURN THE PAGE.

Maurice Buckmaster, head of special operations in France, gives you forged identification papers. He also assigns you a code name to use in messages. You'll be known as Madeleine.

You are also given a French ration card, a tiny single-shot pistol that looks like a pen, and an "L" pill hidden inside a tube of lipstick. "If you can't face torture, take the pill," the chief says. He doesn't need to say that the "L" stands for lethal.

In May 1943 you are given passage into Paris. You meet Emile Garry, head of a Paris resistance group called Prosper, at a safe house.

46

"We are desperate for wireless operators," Garry says. "We need one in St. Quentin and another in Paris."

TO TRAVEL TO ST. QUENTIN,
GO TO PAGE 47.

TO STAY IN PARIS,
TURN TO PAGE 50.

St. Quentin is a factory city and shipping hub just north of Paris. It is guarded by German soldiers. A man named Guy Bieler has built a resistance network. The network's main goal is to derail trains. It is an effective way to disrupt Nazi shipments to their troops. Members of the network are called Musicians. Part of your job will be reporting on the Musicians' activity.

A schoolteacher named Marie Lefevre meets you at the station. She introduces you to Camille Boury, who offers you lodging. Then you meet Odette Gobeaux. You'll be setting up your wireless equipment in her attic.

The attic is drafty but comfortable. You put the wireless on the table and pass the antenna out the window. The antenna transmits radio waves to the receiver in England. Unfortunately its appearance might give you away too. You do your best to disguise the long antenna.

TURN THE PAGE.

You broadcast to London several times a week. Along with information about the Musicians' movements, you send information about German soldiers and their movements. You also pass along messages between the SOE and the Musicians.

"The Musicians will attack railroads at 25 different points, cut phone wires to Paris, and disrupt German communications," you send. "Madeline out."

Messages flow back and forth like chatter over a telephone. "You should be careful," Odette warns. "The Germans have direction-finding units combing the area. They pick up wireless transmissions and follow them to the source." She looks hopeful. "Perhaps you should move to a new location?"

You pretend not to notice her hint. "I'm not worried," you say. In fact, you've never felt so excited or so useful.

Two days later Camille feels a presence behind her as she walks home from the market. She turns in time to see a man slip into an alley. She doesn't see his face, but he's wearing a trench coat with the collar turned up. Is he tracking the wireless? Direction finders can be worn under officers' coats. Or maybe he was just spying on Camille. Either scenario is suspicious.

Camille sends Odette to warn you. This is your second warning. Maybe you should relocate, just to be safe.

TO MOVE, TURN TO PAGE 52.

TO STAY AT YOUR POST, TURN TO PAGE 53.

You're assigned to the Prosper resistance network in Paris. Emile Garry is chief. Your job is to be the messenger between SOE and Prosper.

You stay at a safe house run by Madam Izard. You send three messages a week. At first everything runs well. But six days after you arrive, Nazi secret police officers called the Gestapo arrest almost everyone connected with Prosper.

The Gestapo was formed after Hitler came into power in 1933. Their main job was to find anti-Nazi agents.

Because you are new, you escape their attention. For now you are safe. You tell London about the raid and begin working with two other networks, Cinema and Phono.

"A van has driven past several times," Madam Izard says when you return home from the market one afternoon. "I'm afraid it might be a Gestapo direction-finding van." The vans locate radio signals and lock in on them. Then the Gestapo arrests the operators and confiscates the radio equipment. "Perhaps you should move."

Moving is difficult, and you're comfortable with Madam Izard. You weren't caught last time. Staying means putting her at risk too, but you both knew what you were getting into when you signed up. The decision is yours.

51

TO STAY,
TURN TO PAGE 54.

TO MOVE ON,
TURN TO PAGE 55.

It's time to move on. There's a safe house on the edge of the city near the canal. You transmit one message from the new location before Guy Bieler arrives.

"You've been a great help," he says. "But you must leave France now. It's too risky for you to stay. There's an escape route through Spain. Helpers will guide you, but it will be a difficult journey over the Pyrenees Mountains. We've helped hundreds of French escapees and downed Allied airmen leave that way." He pauses. "But if you are not ready for mountain climbing, the London office will send a plane to collect you. It will take some time. They cannot fly until the moon is full.

TO GO TO SPAIN,
TURN TO PAGE 59.

TO WAIT FOR A PLANE,
TURN TO PAGE 60.

52

You stay at your post. It's a mistake.

Two days later, you are at a café drinking coffee when two armed men arrest you. They are Gestapo, German secret police. They question you over and over, using violence when they think it's necessary.

At first you refuse to talk. But after a while the questions and the taste of blood in your mouth wear you down. Perhaps you should plead innocence. Maybe they will let you go if you're believable enough. Can you tell a convincing lie?

TO ATTEMPT TO LIE, TURN TO PAGE 61.

TO REMAIN SILENT, TURN TO PAGE 63.

It is too much bother to move. It's risky to be seen carrying the heavy wireless around. Besides, facing danger is exciting. You've never felt so energized. You send two more messages from Madam Izard's home.

Things seem to be going well for about a week. But one day when you arrive home, Madam Izard is frantic. "Gestapo officers were here asking questions," she says as she helps you pack. You are sent to Emile Garry's sister, Renee.

TURN TO PAGE 56.

Wireless receivers and transmitters weighed around 30 pounds.

You don't want to put Madam Izard at risk. For two months you move from safe house to safe house, never staying at the same place for more than two or three days. It's inconvenient and you become weary. The wireless set is inconvenient to pack and unpack. Although it's disguised to look like an old suitcase, there's still a risk of being discovered with it out in public. Several times you've had to discourage men who want to help carry your "luggage." You need a more permanent location.

Emile Garry mentions that his sister would be willing to hide you. But perhaps it's time to leave France. The Gestapo seems to be getting closer. There's a path to freedom across the Pyrenees into Spain and on to England.

55

TO FIND EMILE'S SISTER, TURN TO PAGE 56.

TO CROSS THE PYRENEES, TURN TO PAGE 59.

Emile's sister Renee is very welcoming. She shows you where to store the wireless set and tells you to make yourself at home. You feel safer now.

It's a false safety. A few days later you return home to find a strange man in the house. "You're under arrest," he says, drawing a gun.

You fight, trying to remember your training. When that doesn't work you resort to kicking and scratching. You even bite him. When he cries out and clutches his face, it looks like you have a chance to escape. But then another man appears with Gestapo agents close behind. It's all over.

The Gestapo soldiers hold you in an elegant home nearby. They put you on the top floor. A guard arrives to take you for questioning.

"Let me use the bathroom," you demand.

The guard, who seems unfamiliar with female prisoners, agrees.

You lock the door behind you and survey your surroundings. The bathroom window opens onto the roof. You open the window and slip onto a narrow ledge high above the ground.

Several minutes have passed. The guard pounds on the door. "Let's go," he calls. You don't answer.

"Open up!" He knocks again. When there's still no answer, he bursts into the room. It doesn't take him long to figure out where you've gone, and he leans out the window.

"Don't be foolish," he says. "There's nowhere to go out there. You'll fall and break your neck. Come inside."

TO SURRENDER,
TURN TO PAGE 58.

TO STAY ON THE LEDGE,
TURN TO PAGE 68.

You're not afraid to die, but breaking a leg would be a disaster. If the Gestapo questions you when you are in pain, you're likely to reveal secrets. And a broken leg would make future escape attempts impossible. No, it's best to go back inside. Whatever happens, you vow to not give up any information that might help the enemy.

TURN TO PAGE 63.

The path to freedom leads from France over the Pyrenees to Spain. Helpers along the way feed you, give you warm clothing, and hide you from German border guards. They risk their lives to save yours. Several Allied airmen join your group. The mountains are steep. You're cold and tired when you reach sunny Spain.

Spain and Portugal are still neutral. But you're still not safe. Nazi sympathizers report escaping Allies and their helpers to the ever-present Gestapo. You won't be completely safe until you're home. Luckily, your group reaches Lisbon safely and boards a ship to Great Britain.

"You've done well," the SOE chief says. "From now on, you'll work in London." It's been a crazy adventure. But you're happy to be home.

THE
-END-

To follow another path, turn to page 11.
To read the conclusion, turn to page 101.

"I'll wait for the plane," you decide.

"An agent will be in touch," Guy says.

You travel to nearby Angers to wait. Finally an agent named Henri Déricourt makes contact. "I'm sorry," he says apologetically when he picks you up. "We have one stop before the airfield."

One stop? That's no problem.

The car stops in a parking lot. Two men are waiting there. "She's all yours," Déricourt says, pushing you forward. The men are Gestapo. Déricourt is a double agent! How many others has

60 he betrayed? The Gestapo have to hold you back from attacking Déricourt.

The men drive you to their headquarters. You're in the backseat. You remove the lipstick with the L pill inside.

TO TAKE THE PILL,
TURN TO PAGE 64.

TO FACE QUESTIONING,
TURN TO PAGE 65.

They question you again the next day. "What is your name?"

You appear to give in. "I'm Katherine Churchill," you say dramatically. "Please don't tell my uncle Winston that I'm here." It's an outrageous lie. "Uncle Winnie thinks I'm at school in Switzerland. So do my parents. But ... I wanted to see Paris!"

Winston Churchill was the prime minister of Great Britain from 1940–1945 and 1951–1955.

TURN THE PAGE.

The two Gestapo men look at each other. They leave the room. Do they believe you? It's a crazy story—but sometimes crazy is more believable than the truth.

The lie must have worked, because they release you. You're careful on the way back to your safe house, but nobody appears to be following you. When you're sure no one is on your tail, you contact Guy Bieler. He laughs when you tell him what happened. "There's a transport arriving tonight," he says. "Go home to Uncle Winnie."

62

You work at the London SOE office until the war ends. Everyone there calls you Lucky Winnie Churchill. And you are lucky. Many wireless operators never make it home.

THE -END-

To follow another path, turn to page 11.
To read the conclusion, turn to page 101.

They question you, and when you refuse to answer they beat you. You are tired, hungry, and thirsty, but you remain silent. You are transferred to the Gestapo-run prison at Fresnes, south of Paris. Afraid, you blurt out, "I am just a shop girl caught up in this terrible war! Please let me go!"

It's too late. A shop girl would have spoken up sooner. They know you are a spy.

On May 12, 1943, you're moved to Karlsruhe prison, just over the German border. Seven other SOE women go with you, but you are separated once you reach Karlsruhe. The prison is a holding area for captured officers and other military personnel before they are sent to prison camps.

63

Allied bombs drop overhead. You distract yourself by using bits of fabrics and thread from your own clothing to do embroidery.

TURN TO PAGE 67.

You unscrew the lipstick and remove the pill. Your life is probably over either way. You know the location of other resistance networks. You know the codes for the wireless transmissions. Your information would be essential for the Axis.

You place the pill on your back teeth and bite down. You slump in your seat. A Gestapo officer tries to wake you, but it's too late.

By the time the car pulls into Gestapo headquarters, you are dead. After the war ends, you are posthumously awarded the Croix de Guerre, a French military decoration that rewards feats of bravery. It's a great honor. Your family keeps your award on their mantelpiece for guests to see for years to come.

64

THE
-END-

To follow another path, turn to page 11.
To read the conclusion, turn to page 101.

It's harder than you expect to resist. Gestapo agents question you for hours. When you refuse to answer, they beat you.

After several months you're transferred to Ravensbruck, a concentration camp north of Berlin. It's a camp just for women, and there are prisoners from all over Europe. Two young French girls, Yvonne and Lisette, share your cell. The three of you are assigned to a forced labor gang. Every day you dig ditches. Every night you plot an escape.

Lisette is worried. "We will be shot if we fail," she says. Guards in towers with rifles stand waiting to shoot prisoners who run.

"We will die anyway," Yvonne says. "Who will go with me?"

65

TO TRY AN ESCAPE,
TURN TO PAGE 66.

TO STAY IN THE CAMP,
TURN TO PAGE 67.

Escape is your only chance to survive. The work is hard and you're not fed enough. If that's not enough to kill you, the prison guards will. Even little mistakes are enough to earn a beating. Those who are too weak are sent to Uckermark or Auschwitz and never return.

On a rainy April day, a downpour makes the guards careless. You slip into the forest and hide beneath the sheltering branches of a spruce tree.

Ravensbruck was the largest concentration camp for women.

TURN TO PAGE 69.

Life in camp drags on. Many workers become ill from hard labor, little food, and bad water. There are barely enough supplies for soldiers fighting on the front lines; the Germans cannot spare any for political prisoners.

One night a guard pulls you from the barracks. Three other female SOE agents join you. You wonder why you've been rounded up.

After a cramped ride in a cattle car, the train reaches Dachau, a concentration camp in southern Germany. You face more questions. You are beaten, but you never say a word. After days under torture, the questioning stops. You are marched to a wooded area. A guard raises his gun. "Liberté!" you cry. Then he fires.

THE
-END-

To follow another path, turn to page 11.
To read the conclusion, turn to page 101.

It's only a few feet to the next rooftop. You rush toward the edge. The guard fires and misses. You risk a glance back. He's stuck in the window! What a lucky break!

You leap onto the roof, run across, and jump to the next. The houses are close together, making it an easy path. Finally you reach a fire escape. You climb down and jump to the ground. You slip into an alley and hide until nightfall. The dark hides your face and makes it safe to stroll the Paris streets.

You have nothing—no identification, no money, and no way to contact anyone. You walk all night, not knowing where you're headed. All you know is that Paris is no longer a safe place for you to be.

The next day you reach a small village and sneak into the church. The priest hides you in his cellar. Several villagers bring food and blankets. Life in hiding is difficult. You're restless and feel vulnerable. A single person could give away your secret at any time. You're tempted to leave on your own, but that would endanger the village.

Months pass. In April 1945 American troops arrive. You run into the street shouting, "Welcome!" in English. They help you return to London. You lose touch with the others you met in France, but from time to time you remember them and pray for their welfare. You never discuss your war service. When you die in 2010, your neighbors are amazed to learn of your heroism during World War II.

THE
-END-

To follow another path, turn to page 11.
To read the conclusion, turn to page 101.

British Spitfires were present for every battle during World War II. They were used for both air combat and reconnaissance.

CHAPTER 4

SPY IN THE SKY

It's August 24, 1940, and you're about to start your senior year of high school. But war rages on in Europe, and you itch to join in. Your dream is to enlist with the U.S. Army Air Force. You see yourself flying a Spitfire, the very plane being used to fight the Nazis over British skies.

As soon as school ends, you sign up for a program called Sergeant Pilots. You're ordered to report to a civilian flight school for training. You're one of the youngest men there, but you are as smart and eager to learn as anyone. From your first ride as a passenger, you know this is what you were meant to do. You love flying, and you're good at it.

71

TURN THE PAGE.

In May 1943 you're sent to Mt. Farm, a British airbase near Oxford. Your blue Spitfire handles easily and blends in with the sky. It can fly higher, faster, and farther than other planes, and when you fully understand your mission, you realize it is the only plane fit for the job.

"We've removed the guns and installed cameras," the captain explains. "There is a critical need for photographs of Germany and German military installations in Europe. We'll photograph everything that moves in Europe until this war is won."

You'll fly alone into German territory without a single gun for defense. Instead of bullets you'll be armed with cameras. Two are fitted under the wings and another set pointing down through the bottom of the fuselage. They take large images and can focus at 30,000 feet above the target.

The cameras work together in pairs to create 3-D images. "That way the PIs can judge the heights and widths of what's in the image," the commander explains.

"PIs? Private investigators?"

The commander laughs. "No. Photo interpreters. Some of the smartest people in England and America will analyze these photographs and tell us just what the Nazis are doing. It is vital work." He taps his temple. "Brains will win this war. If— and that's a big if—you can take the photos they need to do it."

You pledge to do your best. "We need photos of German dams in the Ruhr Valley," the commander continues. "Destroying the dams will cripple German factories, but bombing is only effective if the dams are full of water." It's a dangerous mission.

TURN THE PAGE.

"But we also need photos of northern France," he says. "There are some odd structures there. We don't know what they are." France is closer, and the assignment seems less dangerous.

an aerial reconnaissance photograph of the Moehne Dam taken in 1943

**TO PHOTOGRAPH THE DAMS,
GO TO PAGE 75.**

**TO GO TO FRANCE,
TURN TO PAGE 78.**

You wake up at 4:00 a.m. and are in the air before 6:00. Your first stop is Bradwell Bay on England's east coast. Several pilots greet you in the sky.

"What unit are you?" they ask over the radio.

"Photo reconnaissance."

"Where are your guns?"

"No guns."

"Where's your fighter escort?"

"I don't have one."

"Where are you going?"

"Germany."

"Good luck," one of the pilots mumbles. You grin and salute before pulling away.

TURN THE PAGE.

You fly toward Germany unarmed and alone. It's a distance of over 400 miles. You cruise at about 340 miles per hour. It's a beautiful, clear morning when you reach Germany's Ruhr Valley. You circle once above the dam and then prepare to take pictures. You must fly a straight and level course for the cameras to function properly. You hit a button and the cameras begin taking photos.

It's freezing cold in the cockpit. Your hands and feet are stiff. At this altitude, the air is around -50 degrees Fahrenheit. You make three passes. You're about to make a fourth when a dirty black ball bursts in front of the windshield. It's flak from German anti-aircraft guns. You put your head down and fly out of range.

But when you look up you see a contrail, the white streak of condensed water left behind by a high-altitude aircraft. It's probably a German Messerschmitt. They are armed with four deadly guns. Has its pilot spotted you? You have only two choices: continue on hoping he doesn't see you, or try to trick him.

The Messerschmitt 109 was
Germany's primary fighting plane.

TO CONTINUE ON,
TURN PAGE 80.

TO TRICK HIM,
TURN TO PAGE 81.

The captain's comment about "odd structures" interests you. What could they be? Another pilot took the first photos, but the sites themselves are a mystery. The photo interpreters are concerned that they can't figure out what the sites are. You want to prove you can be useful to the PIs.

It's just a little over 200 miles to France. German troops occupy France. You'll have to fly past their anti-aircraft guns and then dip low enough to take photos of the domes.

In less than an hour you reach an area of northern France called Wizernes. You fly high near the French coast, out of range of the anti-aircraft guns. Then you descend. Your target is about 3 miles from the town of Saint-Omer.

You fly over the site. A large concrete dome is built into a quarry. You swoop low and take pictures. You have to take the photos from directly above the site while flying a level course. The photos must be overlapping shots in order to show height and depth when viewed through special lenses.

You pass again and take more photos. You wonder if you're close enough. You know getting the right pictures is important, and you want to impress your superiors. Maybe you should fly in for one more low pass.

TO FLY LOWER, TURN TO PAGE 82.

TO FLY BACK TO MT. FARM, TURN TO PAGE 84.

You weave back and forth to avoid leaving a contrail. You push the Spitfire. It's fast. With luck, the Messerschmitt will never see you. You never see him so you assume you're safe. You turn the Spitfire toward England. Just when you begin to relax, anti-aircraft guns start shooting. You hear a loud ping. One of the cameras is hit. It's pure luck on the gunner's part. The cameras are well hidden. Has your trip been worthless?

Air control guides you back to Mt. Farm. You approach the runway and lower the landing gear. It's stuck! You shake the lever and fly over the runway. You flip the plane and fly upside down. Can you shake the wheels loose? No luck.

There's a wheat field in the distance. It would be a safe landing. But the runway is closer.

TO CHOOSE THE FIELD,
TURN TO PAGE 85.

TO CHOOSE THE RUNWAY,
TURN TO PAGE 91.

80

You don't trust blind luck. You try to accelerate to avoid confrontation. But instead of speeding up, the engine backfires. Your speed drops and the German plane closes the distance. There's no doubt now that he's seen you.

You bank the plane hard. Things begin to spin. G-force hits you like a tank. For a short moment, you black out. The instant you regain consciousness, you grab the controls. You complete the turn and head home. You're out of the Messerschmitt's gun range now. It will take him another 10 miles to complete his turn. Your smaller, faster Spitfire won this battle.

Two hours later the captain finds you. The photos were clear. He invites you to visit Medmenham and see the PIs at work. "Or you can go back out for more."

TO SEE THE PIS AT WORK, TURN TO PAGE 86.

TO FLY ANOTHER MISSION, TURN TO PAGE 98.

You take one more pass and dive into the quarry. You are only about 100 feet above the structure. You'll have to pull up before you hit the rock wall at the back of the quarry. You make it—just barely.

But anti-aircraft guns on the ground have spotted you. Shells burst all around you, creating big black puffs of thick flak. You dive and make a sharp turn. Then you increase your altitude and turn in another direction. It's called evasive action, and it's the only way to avoid being hit. You're careful not to fall into a pattern. You climb high and speed away to safety.

Later the captain says that your close-up photo amazes the PIs. "Years from now they'll call it the most daring photograph of the war!" he says, clapping you on the back.

The PIs invite you to visit their base at Medmenham. It sounds interesting, but you know the captain is about to assign another photo recon mission and you're flying high on his praise.

PIs looked at millions of aerial photographs during the war.

TO VISIT THE PIS,
TURN TO PAGE 86.

TO FLY,
TURN TO PAGE 98.

Even though you didn't get as close as you wanted, the PIs are pleased. There's no question that these sites are dangerous. "We think there are rockets involved," one says.

"Several months ago a British pilot photographed an airfield at Peenemünde, a village in northwest Germany," the captain explains. "Then we heard rumors that the Nazis were developing rockets. When the PIs re-examined the photos, they saw the shadow of a rocket. More than 560 Allied aircraft dropped 1,800 tons of bombs on Peenemünde. The village is gone, but these sites in France remain."

84

You take several more photo runs over the mysterious sites. One day you notice something unusual in a grove of trees near the French coast.

TO LOOK CLOSER, TURN TO PAGE 88.

TO IGNORE IT, TURN TO PAGE 90.

You land in the wheat field. The stalks of wheat act like a cushion. Bits of wheat grass and grain fly in the air around you. The propeller blades are broken but you, the cameras, and the rest of the plane are fine. In fact, the photos came out perfectly. Everyone is pleased. You have a day's rest, and then the captain assigns you another mission.

TURN TO PAGE 98.

It's about an hour's journey to Medmenham. A British officer meets you at the door of the stately home that is headquarters of the Photo Interpretation Unit. "We don't often meet the pilots," he says. You've been warned not to reveal anything you see or hear. It's top secret.

Several PIs are at work in the next room. Men and women study the photos, discuss them, and make notes. Some are using 3-D glasses.

"This is difficult work," the officer whispers. "The PIs have to pay attention to detail and concentrate for long periods of time. Our group includes mathematicians, geologists, and archaeologists. They are experts in using small details to create a big picture. We need imaginative people too. We have artists and musicians on the staff. There is even a former Disney employee here."

Several PIs shake your hand, happy to meet the man behind the photographs. They wish you well on your next mission.

"Without the photos our work would be impossible," a woman says. "With them, we can monitor troop movements and identify targets. Commanders in the field are waiting for the secrets that you capture with your cameras. Stay safe!"

"I intend to," you say as you leave. You're more eager than ever to fly another mission.

On your way back to Mt. Farm, the captain mentions that another pilot has noticed something odd in the forests of northern France. "Near the coast," he adds. "We also need photos of Berlin."

TO CHECK THE FRENCH FOREST, TURN TO PAGE 88.

TO FLY TO GERMANY, TURN TO PAGE 93.

You study the grove of trees from the air. At first you see nothing, even when you come in close. On the second pass, you notice odd shapes. There's a building with ramps. It's connected to something that looks like a ski turned on its side. You activate the cameras and make one more pass before flying home. You climb high in order to avoid anti-aircraft guns and you change course frequently, but the skies are quiet.

Two days later the PIs send word that they need more photos of it—whatever it is. You seem to have found something of interest.

You return to northern France and locate two more of the mysterious sites. You fly in for a close shot. A guard on the ground fires his machine gun at you. Bullets hit the wings where your fuel is stored.

You glance at the fuel gauge just as the needle swings to EMPTY. The mechanics told you the Spitfire has a self-sealing fuel tank. You might be all right. But it's hard to ignore the fact that the plane is telling you that the fuel is gone. What should you do?

Early Spitfires could fly at an altitude of 30,000 feet and reached speeds greater than 300 miles per hour.

TO FLY HOME, TURN TO PAGE 95.

TO PREPARE FOR AN EMERGENCY LANDING, TURN TO PAGE 96.

It's cloudy. You're unlikely to get a good photo, so you turn toward England. You're almost home when you notice a German Messerschmitt on your tail. He fires and hits your left wing. The British coast is visible now, but your Spitfire is sputtering. You struggle to keep it level. You radio home to let them know you are coming but that there's trouble.

British anti-aircraft guns begin firing to help you. You hear an explosion as the German's plane is hit. You're able to wobble your way back to Mt. Farm and land safely.

"We can patch it up, don't you worry," a mechanic reassures you. You're flying again the next day. It ends up being just one of your many war adventure stories.

THE
–END–

To follow another path, turn to page 11.
To read the conclusion, turn to page 101.

You've landed on runways dozens of times, but never without the landing gear. You align the nose of the plane with the runway and brace yourself for impact.

The belly of the plane hits hard. The plane hops, then skids, along the runway. There's a loud screeching noise, and you can see sparks flying outside the window. The plane comes to a slow, grinding stop. Runway workers rush over to assist you. You've been so focused that you don't even notice the pain in your right leg until they pry open the door and try to lift you out.

"Medic!" a worker calls. A base medic arrives; your leg is broken. The medical staff carries you out on a stretcher. For now, you're grounded.

TURN THE PAGE.

The captain visits you in the military hospital. "You won't believe it," he says. "But the cameras weren't damaged. You got some great pictures. Tonight we'll bomb the dams."

You return home to Massachusetts to recover. The rest of the war is spent scanning the headlines for news of the Spitfires and wishing that you were back in the air.

THE
-END-

To follow another path, turn to page 11.
To read the conclusion, turn to page 101.

You'll be photographing the city of Berlin. In June the British began conducting bombing raids on the city at night. The Americans bomb during the day. The raids are called Operation Pointblank. It's a constant onslaught, and by now the Germans are on high alert. "We need photos to check the results of our bombing raids," the captain tells you.

Your run is scheduled at dawn, to avoid Allied bombers. As soon as the cameras are loaded with film and the tanks are full of gas, you fly toward Germany.

Clouds roll in as you reach the mainland. You rely on your instruments. You'd like to think that the clouds protect you, but you know better. There's nothing stopping anti-aircraft guns from firing into the clouds, and you'll be flying blind into their path.

TURN THE PAGE.

You fly high above the target sites, take the photos, and return home without incident.

The photos show a destroyed ball bearing factory, as well as a damaged airplane factory. "The bombers are hitting their targets," the captain says.

You make more than 50 flights to Germany through the end of the war. It is dangerous work, but helping the Allies from six miles above the earth is what you do best.

THE
-END-

To follow another path, turn to page 11.
To read the conclusion, turn to page 101.

You trust the mechanics so you fly home. When you reach Mt. Farm, the maintenance crew checks the plane. "There are lots of bullet holes, but the tank worked as promised. It's just the fuel gauge that failed. We'll fix it, patch the holes, and have you ready to fly in a day or two."

Your photos of the ski-shaped structures are rushed to the PIs. It takes time, but eventually they figure out that the Germans are building ramps for pilotless aircraft called VI rockets. They're also called flying bombs.

The Allies start bombing waves to disable them. Four rockets land on British soil before the Allies can destroy them. One hits London, killing six people. But without your photos, the flying bombs may have killed thousands more.

TURN TO PAGE 99.

You're over occupied territory. Any landing has its risks. You could be taken by the enemy or lost in the middle of nowhere. Your worst fear is drowning. Running out of fuel over the English Channel means sure death. It's a long, cold swim back to land, and you've never been a strong swimmer. You fly north along the coast looking for a safe place to ditch the Spitfire.

Aerial photos helped with planning the final offensive against Germany. In 2009 around 4,000 of the 10 million total photos were released to the public.

When you recheck the fuel gauge, you're shocked. The needle is flipping from EMPTY to FULL. Maybe it's faulty. You take the risk and head for home. You're so worried that you don't notice the German Messerschmitt on your tail until he fires at you.

The Messerschmitt's two wing-mounted cannons and two machine guns blast holes in your wings. You hear pings as bullets skip across the cockpit. You struggle to keep the plane in the air, but your hands won't work. Why? Everything is fuzzy. Blood drips down your cheek. You've been hit! You try to radio in but your shaking hands won't obey before you pass out. The plane crashes into the Channel. Lucky for you you're dead before that happens.

THE
-END-

To follow another path, turn to page 11.
To read the conclusion, turn to page 101.

Flying the Spitfire is a pleasure. You know the dangers, but you also know that the rewards are great. The captain sends you along the French coast. "We need photos of every military installation in the area," he says.

Some days clouds make the job impossible and you turn back. Other times you leave in fog and emerge in sunshine. You slip in and out of enemy territory to photograph sites in Belgium, the Netherlands, and Norway. You photograph armies on the move, military supply depots, and air bases. If it's there, you've captured it on camera.

You and other Allied pilots take millions of photographs of enemy territories. Those photos provide information leading up to the invasion at Normandy, France, on June 6, 1944. You continue to spy on Axis forces as they retreat. You shoot the enemy with your cameras, stealing their secrets from high in the sky.

THE -END-

To follow another path, turn to page 11.
To read the conclusion, turn to page 101.

British planes fly over Paris, France.

CHAPTER 5
EYES EVERYWHERE

More than 60 countries participated in World War II. Their soldiers spoke different languages, practiced different customs, and used different military and shipping codes. Agents who could speak another language and could pose as native people in enemy territory were extremely valuable.

Thousands of people worked in the Allied intelligence services as spies. Some were undercover agents; many more analyzed information. They looked at thousands of newspapers, letters, and reports. They examined millions of photographs. They solved complicated codes and translated foreign languages. They waged a secret war against the enemy.

TURN THE PAGE.

The Germans used a special machine called the Enigma to send coded messages. They believed that their code was unbreakable, and used the Enigma for all war-related communication. However, code-breakers were able to crack the code. The fact that the code was broken was extremely classified, and the Germans never found out. The code-breakers' hard work played a major role in the Allies' victory.

Radio transmitters played huge roles in communication during the war.

The Japanese used the Purple machine. The machine sent messages between Tokyo and the Japanese embassies. However, Purple messages did not include military information, so the Allies had no way to learn about the attack at Pearl Harbor before it happened. The messages did supply updates about German and Italian movements, though. Japanese diplomats sent updates to Tokyo on a regular basis.

Breaking these complex codes required a certain kind of mind. Mathematicians, musicians, and artists tended to be good at code breaking. Those who were used to analyzing data and observing were assets too. Code breakers worked throughout the war deciphering messages sent using these machines' codes.

TURN THE PAGE.

Undercover agents risked their lives. Many died, and few were honored during their lives. Now, nearly 75 years later, some of their stories are finally being told.

Richard Sakakida worked as an undercover agent in the Philippines. He and Arthur Komori, both *Nisei* who lived in Hawaii, were recruited before the Pearl Harbor attacks. Both worked with General Douglas MacArthur and served as intelligence officers until the end of the war.

In 1940 Winston Churchill established the Special Operations Executive to work with resisters in Europe. The first agents were men. In 1942 the SOE began recruiting women to serve in France. Noor Inayat Khan was among the first recruited. She served as a wireless operator in Paris. Yolande Beekman, Eileen Nearne, and Denise Bloch also served in France. Of the four, only Eileen Nearne made it home.

Spy pilots helped the Allies prevent or reduce German rocket attacks. They tracked troop movements and supply lines. They verified targets for bombers and the results of bombing attacks. Photo reconnaissance saved thousands of lives.

Spies have been key to every major war. But prior to World War II, only the British had a government agency—M16—charged with intelligence. In 1942 the United States established the Office of Strategic Services (OSS), but it was disbanded after the war. The Central Intelligence Agency (CIA) was created in 1947.

Today the United States and most other nations use intelligence agencies to keep track of what is happening around the world. As situations and threats change, their intelligence strategies change with them.

TIMELINE

1909—The British government establishes the Secret Service Bureau; later the branches M15, M16, and the Secret Intelligence Service (SIS) are formed.

1933—Adolf Hitler comes to power in Germany.

1939—The U.S. Army Signal Corps begins to decipher Code Purple.

SEPTEMBER 1939—German troops invade Poland, starting World War II.

APRIL-MAY 1940—Germany invades Denmark, Norway, France, the Netherlands, Luxembourg, and Belgium.

JUNE 14, 1940—German troops enter Paris.

JULY 1940—The British government creates the Special Operations Executive to train resistance members in Europe; Germany begins bombing London in the Battle of Britain.

SEPTEMBER 1940—Germany, Italy, and Japan unite to form the Axis powers.

JUNE 1941—Germany invades the Soviet Union.

DECEMBER 1941—Japan bombs the U.S. fleet in Pearl Harbor, Hawaii. The United States, Canada, and Great Britain declare war on Japan. Germany and Italy declare war on the United States.

JANUARY 1942—Japanese forces capture Manila in the Philippines; General MacArthur withdraws to Bataan.

JUNE 1942—The United States forms its own spy agency, the OSS.

JUNE 1944—Allies stage the D-Day invasion of Normandy in France.

FEBRUARY 1945—U.S. forces land on Iwo Jima, off the coast of Japan.

MAY 1945—Germany surrenders to the Allies.

AUGUST 1945—U.S. drops two atomic bombs on Japan.

SEPTEMBER 1945—Japan signs surrender papers, ending World War II.

1947—President Harry Truman creates the CIA.

OTHER PATHS TO EXPLORE

In this book you've seen how the events experienced during World War II look different from three points of view.

Perspectives on history are as varied as the people who lived it. You can explore other paths on your own to learn more about what happened. Seeing history from many points of view is an important part of understanding it.

Here are ideas for other World War II points of view to explore:

+ After Japan bombed Pearl Harbor, more than 100,000 Japanese Americans were arrested and sent to internment camps. Two-thirds of those affected were *Nisei*, born in the United States. Their possessions were taken from them. Some were deported to Japan. How would you feel if the only country you had known turned against you?

+ Several American and British spies spent the war inside Germany posing as Nazi sympathizers. How do you think neighbors and friends would react to learning someone they knew sided with the Nazis?

+ German spies who parachuted into England were often caught and offered a choice: become a double agent or face execution. At one point, the British had about 120 double agents. What are some of the challenges those agents might have faced?

READ MORE

Bearce, Stephanie. *Top Secret Files: World War II: Spies, Secret Missions, & Hidden Facts from World War II.* Waco, Texas: Prufrock Press, Inc., 2015.

Burgan, Michael. *World War II Spies: An Interactive History Adventure.* North Mankato, Minn.: Capstone Press, 2013.

Hopkinson, Deborah. *Courage & Defiance: Stories of Spies, Saboteurs, and Survivors in World War II Denmark.* New York: Scholastic Press, 2015.

INTERNET SITES

FactHound offers a safe, fun way to find Internet sites related to this book. All of the sites on FactHound have been researched by our staff.

Here's all you do:
Visit *www.facthound.com*
Type in this code: 9781491478851

GLOSSARY

blockade (blok-AYD)—a closing off of an area to keep people or supplies from going in or out

civilian (si-VIL-yuhn)—a person who is not in the military

decipher (de-SY-fur)—breaking a code that uses letters or symbols to represent letters of the alphabet

detention center (di-TEN-shuhn SEN-tur)—a place where people suspected of a crime are held

evacuate (i-VA-kyuh-wayt)—to leave an area during a time of danger

flak (FLAK)—anti-aircraft fire

forge (FORJ)—to make an illegal copy of paintings, money, or other valuable objects

fuselage (FYOO-suh-lahzh)—the main body of an airplane

G-force (JEE FORSS)—the force of gravity on a moving object

interrogate (in-TER-oh-gate)—to question someone

Morse code (MORSS KODE)—a method of sending messages by radio using a series of long and short clicks

reconnaissance (ree-KAH-nuh-suhnss)—a mission to gather information about an enemy

BIBLIOGRAPHY

History of WW2: Code Breaking. History.co.uk. 30 April 2015. http://www.history.co.uk/study-topics/history-of-ww2/code-breaking

Japanese-American Internment. U.S. History. 13 April 2015. http://www.ushistory.org/us/51e.asp

Kross, Peter. *The Encyclopedia of World War II Spies.* Fort Lee, N.J.: Barricade, 2001.

Noor Inayat Khan: The Indian Princss Who Spied for Britain. BBC. 26 April 2015. http://www.bbc.com/news/uk-20240693

O'Toole, G. J. A. *The Encyclopedia of American Intelligence and Espionage.* New York: Facts On File, 1988.

Rogers, James T. *The Secret War: Espionage in World War II.* New York: Facts on File, 1991.

Sulik, Michael J. *Spying in America: Espionage from the Revolutionary War to the Dawn of the Cold War.* Washington, D.C.: Georgetown U. P., 2012.

War of Secrets: Cryptology in WWII. National Museum of the US Air Force. 30 April 2015. http://www.nationalmuseum.af.mil/factsheets/factsheet.asp?id=9722

INDEX